Flowers

with **Southern Lady**®

The Language of Flowers

Flowers

with Southern Lady

hm | books

contents

seasonal beauty

Whether it's a formal centerpiece of fragrant roses and frilly peonies arranged in a silver bowl for a formal dinner or a handful of fresh-picked daisies tucked into a simple Mason jar at a birthday party, floral displays are an integral part of any occasion. They are just as important to a setting as the china and linens—and the table would be bare without them!

At *Southern Lady,* we wholeheartedly believe in the invaluable contribution of flowers, and that's why whenever you see a setting in our magazine, you'll always find exquisite florals at the heart of it. We love how an arrangement brings instant color and personality to the table, the way it complements the other elements, or underscores a theme. For years now, our readers have been telling us that we inspire them with the gorgeous floral designs throughout our pages, so we knew we had to corral these wonderful ideas into one beautiful book. *Flowers with Southern Lady* not only offers dozens of dazzling settings, it also includes how-tos for creating your own displays and some of our favorite go-to resources. Even aspiring home florists will be able to create stunning arrangements with the inspiration and instructions found within.

So, whether you purchase flowers from your favorite florist or clip blossoms from your own garden, you'll find all the help you need for arranging your own amazing creations in no time at all!

All our best to you,
The *Southern Lady* staff

"The seasons are what a symphony ought to be: four perfect movements in harmony with each other."

—Arthur Rubenstein

Ode to *Spring*

Bright and cheery blossoms dance across the table in a spirited tribute to the season devoted to rebirth and renewal.

Spring may tiptoe in one tulip at a time, but before long, it's as if the whole world is in bloom, and we are caught up in the exuberance of it all. Like a turning kaleidoscope, colors collide in botanical displays that leave us oohing and ahhing in amazement. The season brings so many reasons to celebrate, and each one is made all the more special with the beauty of fresh flowers. From birthday parties in the backyard to informal gatherings on the porch to Easter dinners around the table, flowers add personality and panache to any occasion. With many of the components available from our own gardens, fabulous floral arrangements are just a few steps—and snips—away.

RIGHT: As the perfect accompaniment with a family Easter meal, fill a large vase or bowl with fresh-cut stems of hydrangeas, roses, ranunculuses, bicolored tulips, and pink waxflowers, adding maidenhair fern for filler.

BELOW: On either side of the main centerpiece, place a pair of small baskets filled with the same flowers to finish this salvo of spring.

avian attraction

Capture the colors of spring with a vibrant arrangement that combines hot pink tea roses, orange-tipped bicolor roses, deep pink ranunculuses, and lime green Bells of Ireland—with a faux flier flitting about—for a centerpiece worthy of the season.

OPPOSITE: In addition to the centerpiece, give each guest a personal posy by filling a tiny flowerpot with one large rose and surrounding that with a half dozen smaller bicolor buds. Fill in around the rim with 'Gold Mound' sedum and green reindeer moss.

chasing rainbows

Rather than mixing blooms into one large arrangement, separate them by shades.
Place a medley of containers down the middle of the table, starting with lime-green
chrysanthemums, followed by purple irises, pink tulips, and ending with yellow
roses and ranunculuses.

Celebrate the sheer exhilaration of spring with a sumptuous arrangement anchored by orange roses, raspberry tulips, and shell pink poppies. Fill in with stock, rex begonia leaves, and jasmine vine. Placed in a purple transferware bowl, this display is sure to lend loads of charm to any occasion.

For a simple but charming centerpiece, invert an assortment of stemmed glassware over single blossoms, like the roses and alstroemeria shown here. Then, place a votive candle atop each upended base.

Trim the stems of a dozen blush roses, and place in a pretty bowl, filling in with magnolia leaves.

"*I* *must have flowers,*
always and always."

—Claude Monet

For floral delights on a small scale, tuck white waxflowers and hypericum berries into pretty containers, like these sweet little bird vases, shown here. Or, choose a sugar bowl in pink Depression glass for a nosegay composed of white roses and hypericum berries.

ABOVE: This sweet springtime medley of white blossoms is nestled in a woven basket. It is composed of anemones, tulips, hydrangeas, lilies, snapdragons, and gerbera daisies with dark centers, and cradles a stone bird figurine among the blooms.

OPPOSITE: Oftentimes, the simplest things are also the most striking. For a clean and classic design that fits the bill, stand stems of white lilies in a pink Depression glass pitcher.

Summer Serenade

The sheer abundance of blooms fills this season
with color and fragrance to delight the senses and
tickle every floral fancy.

Nothing quite compares to a summer garden in full
bloom. Fluffy mophead hydrangeas bend to shelter shade-loving hostas, while
climbing roses ramble over stone walls and trellises. Sweet potato vines and
trailing petunias tumble from patio pots, and brilliantly hued fuchsia drips from
hanging baskets. The heady perfume of white jasmine mingles with those of
Southern magnolias and sweet gardenias for a sentimental scent that defines the
season and lingers in the memory long after summer has faded to fall. For those of
us who have spent countless hours planning, planting, and nurturing our botanical
babies, this season is the culmination of all our devotion, and to create floral
arrangements with the fruits of our labor is an incomparable delight.

All the makings for a gorgeous centerpiece lie in the backyard garden—pink hydrangeas, red roses, gerbera daisies, dark pink peonies, and yellow yarrow. Fill in with English ivy, variegated hosta leaves, or anything else that strikes your fancy.

ABOVE: For pretty-as-you-please place card holders, slip guests' names into tiny gilded birdcages filled with nosegays of the same flowers in the centerpiece.

OPPOSITE: Fill a pretty silver teapot with pink hydrangeas and waxflowers, red roses, bicolored gerbera daisies, dark pink peonies, and yellow yarrow, along with English ivy and variegated hosta leaves, for this cheery arrangement.

RIGHT: A medley of favorite spring blossoms—roses, dahlias, snapdragons, celosia, and more—combine with hanging amaranthus and dusty miller for a beautiful seasonal centerpiece, arranged in a striking majolica bowl.

BELOW: When hosting an outdoor gathering, set up a beverage station for the convenience of guests. A simple cart will do, but make it party-worthy with an arrangement of roses, zinnias, and lavender placed in a pretty pitcher.

ABOVE: For spring place cards, inscribe plant markers with guests' names, and place in wheat grass planted in votives.

OPPOSITE: Anchor a seasonal arrangement with early-blooming hydrangeas in deep shades of purple and pink, adding a few stems of flowers and foliage for contrast.

Echo the hues of colorful woven baskets by planting with bright flowers, such as yellow rudbekias, red and yellow celosia, orange and pink petunias, and white and purple angelonias.

Scoop out the fruit from half a watermelon, and fill with gerbera daisies and *Nemesia*, along with hydrangeas, red begonias, Queen Anne's lace, creeping fig, and stock for the perfect summer display.

ABOVE: Bring the vivid hues of the garden to the table with daylilies, gerbera daisies, roses, snapdragons, and hydrangeas. They make for a cheery bouquet when tucked in a charming container.

OPPOSITE: Stand this summery bouquet of gerbera daisies in a pretty vase that captures the soft aqua shade of translucent sea glass.

summer at the shore

The beautiful blues and greens that are synonymous with the sea are as cool and calming as an ocean breeze. Let coastal colors inspire a setting anchored by aqua-hued dinnerware. Frosting spray turns ordinary bottles and jelly jars into translucent vases reminiscent of sea glass.

Fill some of the frosted bottles and jars with candles, some with white sand, and others with white lisianthuses and branchlets of green leaves to create a simple yet dazzling centerpiece.

Arrange tall palm fronds and Bells of Ireland stems in a milky glass vase, and surround them with hydrangea blooms, allowing the leaves to fan out over the top of the vase.

Homage to *Fall*

The burnished shades of autumn lend their
warmth and glow in the form of beautiful flowers
and foliage to settings indoors and out.

$\mathcal{T}he\ dazzling\ hues$ of autumn leaves as they transition from green to gold, orange, and scarlet are an amazing display to be sure, but the leaves aren't the only show in town. Fall offers much in the way of flowers that are just as colorful as their leafy companions. Fields of sunflowers wave in the breeze, and roadsides are dotted with bright yellow goldenrod and purple asters. Mums and witch hazel lend their cheery charm to gardens where sweet autumn clematis spills like a fragrant waterfall and red spider lilies turn their frilly faces to the sun. Some of the prettiest arrangements combine the beauty of both flowers and foliage for a true tribute to this prismatic season.

Go all out with an arrangement that celebrates the harvest hues of fall. Yellow cymbidium orchids, peach roses, Annabelle hydrangeas, dusty miller, and pepperberries are the main components of the design, which also features fall foliage as filler.

"*Autumn . . . the year's last loveliest smile.*"

—William Cullen Bryant

Set a table for two beside the lake, complete with a lovely tiered arrangement that suits the season. Bronze chrysanthemums and pale green hydrangeas, along with fall berries and foliage, are nestled in metallic bowls that sit atop a silver beaded-rim cake stand.

alfresco setting

Revel in the beautiful fall weather with a table set under the oaks. The setting elements marry dressy with casual, so create floral designs that have the same feel by mixing elegant Quicksand roses with blue thistles, dusty miller, and maple leaves.

RIGHT: In lieu of one large centerpiece, tuck smaller bouquets in three antique silver bud vases—with the middle vase slightly taller than the other two—and arrange them on a silver platter, along with fall fruit and a few loose thistles.

BELOW: Pair roses and a hydrangea bloom in a small silver basket for a sweet nosegay that complements the larger arrangements.

ABOVE: Peach roses may signify modesty, but this arrangement that blends those blooms with hydrangeas, hypericum berries, setaria grass, and asparagus fern is definitely a big show-off. Other elements, such as magnolia cones and fall foliage, add texture to the mix.

OPPOSITE: Bring the harvest hues of the season to the table with a centerpiece featuring flowers mixed with pumpkins, pears, and Indian corn placed on a burlap runner.

Fold in all the favorite colors of fall with an extravagant centerpiece arranged in a pretty ceramic bowl. Mix stems of orange calla lilies with deep red dahlias, rose hips, orange kangaroo paw, flame vine, clover, and dried seed pods, along with Italian ruscus, and other greenery.

What a wonderful way to welcome guests to your home! Tuck a mix of sunflowers, snapdragons, and roses in a cone-shaped door basket. Fill in with small apples, hanging amaranthus, cedar sprigs, and more. And for a dash of panache—feathers!

Choose a handsome pottery bowl for a container, and fill it with a prismatic array of autumn flowers, such as chrysanthemums, button mums, Queen Anne's lace, orange waxflowers, and others—the brighter, the better.

ABOVE: Peach roses, ruby dahlias, and dusky pink cymbidium orchids star in an arrangement that also contains stems of golden craspedia, hypericum berries, and a variety of succulents inserted in soaked floral foam.

OPPOSITE: This wee display of yellow roses, dusty miller, thistles, and trailing ivy offers a sweet note to a vignette tucked among the shelves.

Winter Wonderland

Flowers brighten every occasion in this season of celebrations, whether it's a joyful holiday gathering or a romantic dinner for two.

When the shivery winds begin to blow and the landscape becomes an icy ode to the neutrals of winter, it's nice to borrow a bit of spring with vibrant floral arrangements that warm our homes and lift our spirits. From beautiful centerpieces and tiny vignettes to Christmas décor that shines from table to tree to mantel, flowers bring splashes of color at the time of year we need their happy countenance the most. Whether you underscore the signature red and green of the season with scarlet roses and greenery or put your own spin on holiday displays with deep purple calla lilies and lime green Bells of Ireland, flowers are certain to turn a gray day to a sunny one in a snap.

RIGHT: Magnolia leaves offer twice the beauty—one side is a shiny deep green and the other a soft bronze. Connect branches with florist wire to create a garland and mini wreath for the mantel.

BELOW: To dress up a Christmas package, center a pretty ornament in a sprig of magnolia leaves, and attach to the ribbon with a twist of wire.

dress up the holidays

The bright pop of crimson roses adds a formal note to any arrangement, and this mantel adornment underscores that idea. A trio of vases filled with roses and pepperberries stands out among boxwood boughs. For an eye-catching centerpiece, mix roses with red orchids and tulips, along with pink alstroemerias and pepperberries.

ABOVE: Turn an ordinary green houseplant into a seasonal centerpiece with a few festive additions. Simply slip stems of red roses into the soil around the center of the plant, as shown, and surround them with glittery ball ornaments and matching bows on either side.

OPPOSITE: Clip boxwood branches and stems of holly berries from the yard, and combine them with red roses in a slender vase. Slip into a larger vase and fill in with ornaments.

"*Arranging a bowl of flowers in the morning can give a sense of quiet in a crowded day—like writing a poem or saying a prayer.*"

—Anne Morrow Lindbergh

Though the same white hydrangeas and calla lilies are used in this sideboard vignette, the look is quite different from the preceding arrangement. Gather a grouping of brass vases, and fill each with these beautiful blooms, adding sprigs of cedar to fluff.

Tuck a single calla lily and hydrangea in a tiny vase, and tie to a package with tulle ribbon.

Dried elements—
winterberries, green
craspedia balls,
and white reindeer
moss—combine with
hypericum berries for
a striking arrangement.

Fashion this ode to
nature by placing
ivory dahlias and
winterberries in a
clear vase, and filling
in with a variety of
foliage, vines, and
bare branches.

Perfect for Christmas—or Valentine's Day—a lovely arrangement of pristine white roses surrounded by bright red hypericum berries is tucked into a pink footed container. The elements are simple, but the result is stunning.

Pair the rose and berry display with a fresh greenery garland and an oversize wreath. Echo the colors of the arrangement with pink and red ribbon threaded through the wreath and tied to mercury glass ornaments on the mantel.

Pink flowers add panache to a sophisticated setting in gold and ivory. Carry the rosy theme from the centerpiece to the Christmas tree by decorating a white-flocked fir with twinkle lights and silky ornaments in a creamy hue. Loop yards of shimmery pink ribbon through the branches, and top the tree with a bow, allowing the ends to trail like tendrils down the tree.

Give the illusion of twice the size—and twice the beauty—of an arrangement of red roses and pink peonies by placing it in front of a mirror. Or try a refined rustic design of roses, snapdragons, and assorted greenery set in a birch wood vase.

Notes & How-tos

Here's a helpful guide to get you started on your creative floral endeavors.

An afternoon spent puttering around in a potting
shed is a true joy for many Southern ladies, even if the shed is actually just an area
set aside on the patio. It's important to have all the necessary tools close at hand,
but it's also fun to create a space that reflects a gardener's personality and offers
inspiration as well. Visit flea markets and tag sales to find pre-loved dining tables,
benches, and other pieces of furniture that can stand in as a worktable, shelves,
and organizers for seed packets, tools, and twine. Old enamel mixing bowls come
in handy for starting seedlings and stirring up potting-soil mixtures. Imagine the
many pleasant hours ahead for this lucky green-thumb enthusiast!

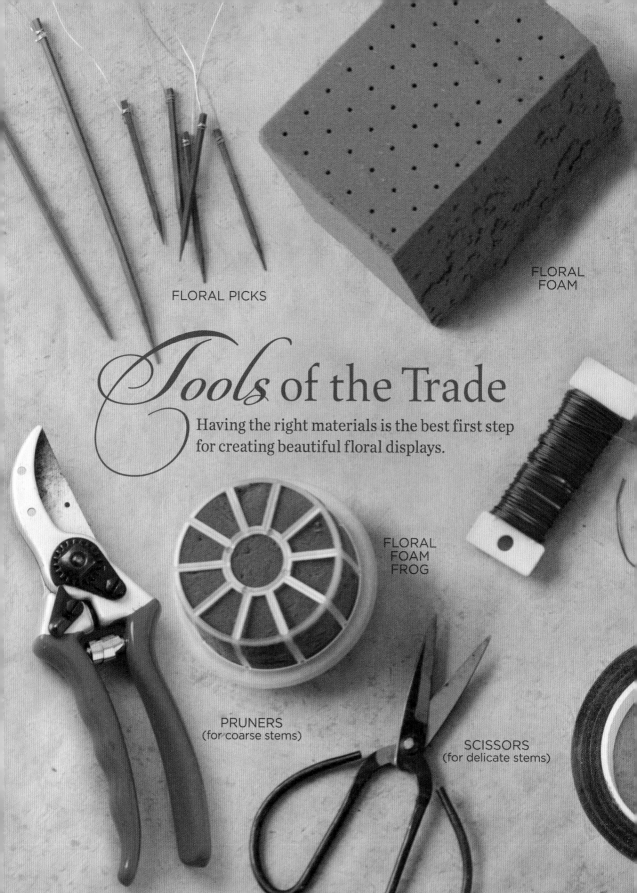

FLORAL PICKS

FLORAL FOAM

Tools of the Trade

Having the right materials is the best first step
for creating beautiful floral displays.

FLORAL FOAM FROG

PRUNERS
(for coarse stems)

SCISSORS
(for delicate stems)

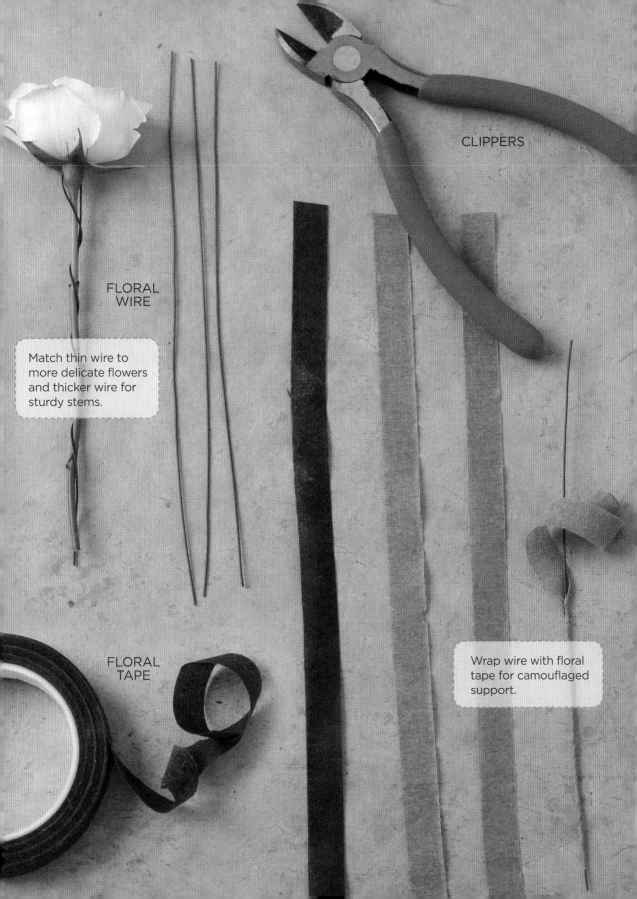

CLIPPERS

FLORAL
WIRE

Match thin wire to
more delicate flowers
and thicker wire for
sturdy stems.

FLORAL
TAPE

Wrap wire with floral
tape for camouflaged
support.

Helpful Tips
for Creating Beautiful Arrangements

Here are some ideas to make your floral endeavors a bit easier:

FLOWER CONDITIONING

To ensure long-lasting displays, conditioning is a must! Here's how:

❧ Cut the flower stems at a 45-degree angle, and remove any foliage that will fall below the water line.

❧ Place flowers in a clean bucket or deep container with 4-5 inches of room-temperature water. Store in a cool location overnight.

❧ Once the flowers are conditioned, blooms and stems will be stronger and better able to hold up during arranging.

❧ Always use a clean vase, and keep the arrangement fresh by changing the water daily.

GRIDS & ARMATURES
FOR ARRANGING

Try these options for forming the foundation for arrangements:

PIN CUSHION, KENZAN, FLORAL FROG
Pros:
- works in a variety of container sizes
- allows fresh water to reach flowers
- creates a looser and more natural arrangement
- can be reused

Cons:
- more expensive
- more difficult to use because the frog will not anchor some stems

FLORAL FOAM
Pros:
- works in a variety of container shapes
- holds flowers securely in place for transport

Cons:
- more expensive
- some flowers do not absorb water well

HAND TIED (USING WATERPROOF TAPE, RUBBER BAND, OR WIRE)
Pros:
- design comes together faster than with other methods
- easier to change water

Cons:
- more difficult for inexperienced designers
- flowers cannot be moved around once they are bound in place

CHICKEN WIRE
Pros:
- provides a very sturdy grid for flowers
- holds flowers securely for transport
- good for supporting the heavy stems of large arrangements

Con:
- wire shows with clear vases, so opaque containers are advised

CLEAR TAPE GRID
Pros:
- provides a fairly sturdy grid
- does not show on clear containers
- grid size can be small or large
- allows fresh water to reach flowers

Cons:
- time-consuming to make
- grid can fall apart if stems are rearranged too much

CURLY WILLOW GRID
PROS:
- offers a natural look
- quick to make
- willow branches have a natural acid that fights bacteria growth

Con:
- more difficult to place stems exactly where you want

One way to facilitate flower arranging is with a floral frog. Placed in the bottom of a vase or bowl, this handy apparatus keeps stems anchored in place while allowing accessibility to water. Frogs come in a variety of sizes and materials, such as glass, ceramic, or bronze, and can be found at florist and garden shops.

Spring

"Spring makes
its own statement, so
loud and clear that the
gardener seems to be only
one of the instruments,
not the composer."

—Rainer Maria Rilke

Basket of Beauties

This bunny-approved arrangement builds on a base of cabbage heads and is filled with pretty spring blooms. Rest assured, it will delight people, too!

WHAT YOU NEED:
Plastic-lined basket
Floral foam
Florals: pink and orange ranunculuses, pink tulips, viburnum,
    cabbage heads

HOW TO MAKE:
ONE: Soak floral foam with water, and place in the bottom of a plastic-lined basket. (The green foam adds to the illusion of flowers emerging from grass.)

TWO: Using flower shears, trim viburnum boughs, as shown, leaving woody stems about 3 inches in length.

THREE: Trim any damaged outer leaves from three heads of cabbage. Insert one head in the center of the floral foam, and one head in each end.

FOUR: Fill in around the cabbage with stems of viburnum. Leave ample space down the center to insert stems of ranunculuses and tulips until the basket is full.

1

2

3

Blooms Under Glass

What could be simpler—or more elegant—than a trio of tulip blossoms captured under stemmed glassware that does double duty as lovely candleholders?

WHAT YOU NEED:
Waterproof rectangular tray with lip
Three tall footed hurricane or pilsner glasses
Short pillar candles
Florals: white tulips

HOW TO MAKE:
ONE: Insert one tulip, bloom side down, into a glass to determine where to cut stems. Cut the stem at a right angle, so that it will take up water once it is in place; repeat with the other two tulips.

TWO: Pour water in the tray, filling to the rim.

THREE: Turn glasses upside down, and position over the water in the tray so that each flower stem touches the water. Place candles atop the upended bases of the glasses.

Summer

"Summer afternoon—
summer afternoon;
to me those have always
been the two most
beautiful words in the
English language."

—Henry James

1

2

3

4

5

6

Floral tape can be a gardener's best friend. Use it to secure fresh-cut blooms from the garden to strengthen the stems and hold them in place while trimming the ends.

Melon Bouquet

A farmers'-market favorite combines with bright and beautiful summer flowers for an arrangement that celebrates the season's bounty.

WHAT YOU NEED:

Watermelon
Large Mason jar
Floral tape
Florals: zinnias, red and white anemones, hydrangeas, hosta leaves

HOW TO MAKE:

ONE: Trim one end of a watermelon to allow it to stand. Cut other end so that the melon is the height of the jar.

TWO: Place the melon on a plate or in a bowl. Scoop the fruit from the melon.

THREE: Place the jar in the melon; stuff with a plastic bag to hold the jar in place.

FOUR: Create a hand-tied bouquet of flowers, finishing with hosta leaves to form a collar; secure with floral tape.

FIVE: Trim stems to fit inside the jar.

SIX: Place bouquet in the jar, and add water.

Reach for the Stars

Welcome in the season with a basketful of flowers that combines a mix of textures and colors for an eye-catching display.

WHAT YOU NEED:
Plastic-lined basket
Dried moss
Florals: hydrangeas, fernleaf lavender, creeping fig

HOW TO MAKE:
ONE: Leaving the plants in the pots, arrange the three components in the basket, as shown.

TWO: Layer the dried moss around the plants, tucking it in so that the creeping fig cascades over the moss and down the basket.

Fall

"Autumn is a second spring when every leaf is a flower."

—Albert Camus

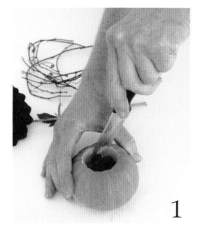

1

2

3

Pumpkin Posies

Create individual tabletop arrangements that double as exquisite place card holders with autumn's favorite squash and frilly flowers.

WHAT YOU NEED:
Mini pumpkins, one per place setting
Grapevine
Florals: dahlias

HOW TO MAKE:
ONE: Cut a silver-dollar size hole around the pumpkin stem, taking care not to puncture the bottom; carefully scoop out and dispose of inside matter.

TWO: Fill interior of each pumpkin with water.

THREE: Cut a dahlia stem to fit, and place in a pumpkin. Fashion the grapevine into a wreath slightly larger that the circumference of the pumpkin. Center the wreath on a plate, and top with a pumpkin. Repeat for additional pumpkins.

Natural Beauty

Borrow a brilliant idea from Mother Nature, and create a container wrapped in birch bark and tied with twine to hold a colorful fall arrangement.

WHAT YOU NEED:

Large Mason jar
Sheet of birch bark from the crafts store
Twine
Florals: tulips, peach stock, cotinus branches, seeded eucalyptus

HOW TO MAKE:

ONE: Gather supplies.

TWO: Trim birch bark to fit all the way around the Mason jar.

THREE: Cut a length of twine that will wrap around the jar several times, and tie off.

FOUR: Add the components, beginning with the seeded eucalyptus to form a base for the flowers.

FIVE: Trim all but the top few leaves from the stems of the peach stock. Place in jar.

SIX: To finish the design, add the tulips, arranging them so that they arc artfully over the container.

Peach blossoms are a great addition to floral displays because of their sturdy stems and frilly flowers. They are often used in Japanese Ikebana arrangements.

1

2

3

Gracious Greeting

Start the warm welcome at the front door with a cheery hanging basket of beautiful autumn flowers and colorful foliage.

WHAT YOU NEED:
Door basket
Two Mason jars
Florals: assorted dahlias, clematis vine, branches of nandina,
   Bradford pear, and Virginia creeper with blue berries

HOW TO MAKE:
ONE: Place Mason jars in the basket, and fill with water. Cut clematis and fall branches, removing any foliage that may fall below the water line. Place in the water to form a sturdy base in which to insert flowers.

TWO: Cut dahlias slightly longer than base foliage so that stems and blooms are supported. Cut nandina slightly longer than dahlias, and insert.

THREE: Complete arrangement by adding the Virginia creeper with berries. Secure the basket to the door.

Winter

"*Christmas waves a magic wand, and behold, everything is softer and more beautiful.*"

—Norman Vincent Peale

Holiday Array

The season's signature shades of red and green combine to create a formal arrangement that adds a pop of color to any setting.

WHAT YOU NEED:
Waterproof shallow bowl
Flower frog/kenzan
Florals: assortment of red roses and spray roses, ilex branches with berries

HOW TO MAKE:
ONE: Remove thorns and leaves from roses. Trim stems to a length of 3-4 inches.

TWO: Arrange by placing the upright roses in the flower frog.

THREE: Tuck in the lower stems at an angle, filling the bowl.

FOUR: Finish the arrangement by filling in with the ilex branches that have been trimmed to a length that allows them to sit about 3 inches above the roses.

Petite Posy

Even the tiniest of arrangements can make a big splash, just like this sweet seasonal design tucked in a silver cream pitcher.

WHAT YOU NEED:
Cream pitcher
Florals: red ranunculuses, green berzillia branches, juniper or cedar sprigs

HOW TO MAKE:
ONE: Place sprigs of juniper or cedar in a small silver pitcher.

TWO: Add three bunches of berzillia branches, as shown.

THREE: Add stems of ranunculuses to finish off this delightful little display.

index

*"And Spring arose on the garden fair,
Like the Spirit of Love felt everywhere."*

—Percy Bysshe Shelley